FARM

BY K.C. KELLEY

AMICUS READERS ● AMICUS INK

Amicus Readers and Amicus Ink are imprints of Amicus
P.O. Box 1329, Mankato, MN 56002
www.amicuspublishing.us

Cataloging-in-Publication Data is on file with the Library of Congress.
ISBN 978-1-68151-305-8 (library binding)
ISBN 978-1-68152-261-6 (paperback)
ISBN 978-1-68151-341-6 (eBook)

Editor: Sara Frederick
Designer: Patty Kelley
Photo Researcher/Producer: Shoreline Publishing Group LLC

Photo Credits:
Cover: st-fotograf/Dreamstime.com
Adobe Stock: Wckiw 12, Diyanadimitrova 15,
Dreamstime.com: Noam Armonn 4, Darren Baker 6, Citalliance 8, Anke Van Wyk 11, Jake Pignanello 16BR, Taina Sohlman 16TL, Vlasta Handlir 16TR, Giovanni Triggiani 16BL. Shutterstock: Holbox 3.

Printed in China.

HC 10 9 8 7 6 5 4 3 2 1
PB 10 9 8 7 6 5 4 3 2 1

Where does our food come from?
Let's visit a farm and find out.

Farms grow lots of food.
Andy helps pick lettuce.

Some farms
have trees.
Dana picks apples.

Big farms grow
wheat and corn.
Brenna finds a
fresh ear of corn.

Animals live
on farms.
Chickens lay eggs.
Cows give milk.
Zena feeds a horse.

Farmers work hard.
They have to
dig in the soil.
Here's Danny
pulling some weeds!

That was a great day on the farm. Let's go eat what we picked!

THINGS TO SEE ON A FARM

tractor

goat

barn

hay bale